THE WEIGHT
OF WHAT'S *GONE*

Jenna Lowthert

the weight of what's gone
jenna lowthert

the weight of what's gone
jenna lowthert

ACKNOWLEDGMENTS

The Weight of What's Gone would not have come to life without the encouragement of the amazing people who have joined my grief community over the years.

Your shared stories, your raw emotions, and your messages of gratitude have been a light and motivation to compile my collection of words on grief and loss into a book.

Thank you for allowing me to share my heart and my story with you. Every word, on every page, holds a piece of the pain I have felt on my grief journey.

This book is *for you, for us..*
and for the ones that we will never forget.

-

Sometimes, the greatest things we do, are the things we don't even realize we are doing. Let the light you give shine brightest in the hearts of those you never even knew were in the dark.

-

www.daughterofanangel.com

the weight of what's gone
jenna lowthert

the weight of what's gone
jenna lowther

INTRODUCTION

If you are holding this book in your hands, you have most likely lost someone that meant so much to you.. and I am *so* sorry for that.

Grief is something I never thought I'd understand so deeply until I lost my 48-year-old mother to stage four lung cancer when I was just 24.

In that moment, everything around me changed in ways I couldn't describe. Life looked so different for me and I had to find a way to cope and navigate this world without the most important person to me.

This book is my way of putting words to the feelings that so many of us hold but can't always express.

Grief is heavy, but so is love..
and somehow, *we learn to carry the weight of both.*

Through quotes and poems, I share with you my perspective on grief and the rawness of all that comes with it.

This isn't just about loss—it's about the love that remains for the people we lost.

I hope my words bring you comfort, a sense of understanding, or at the very least, a reminder that you *are never alone.*

the weight of what's gone
jenna lowthert

the weight of what's gone
jenna lowthert

the weight of
what's gone
is not only
in the sadness.

sometimes it's in
the realization
that some things
will never be
the same again.

the weight of what's gone
jenna lowthert

what i have learned about grief
is that we keep on going..

> *even when we*
> *think we can't.*

the weight of what's gone
jenna lowthert

their shoes still by the door.
their favorite mug,
still on the kitchen counter.
all their things,
just as they left them.

frozen in time.

it's as if they are just out for the day
and will be coming back sometime soon
but life doesn't give us that courtesy
and the silence reminds us that they
won't be returning home..

..and i think that is what hurts the most.

the weight of what's gone
jenna lowthert

every time you smile,
they are smiling with you.

every time you cry,
they are holding you so tight,
even if you cannot see them.

the love you shared doesn't end
just because they are no longer here.

it will forever live on in you,
in the choices you make,
in the kindness you show and
in the strength you find to keep going,
despite all the heartache and
sadness that missing them brings.

the weight of what's gone
jenna lowthert

how unfair it is,

that i have to live
the rest of my life,

without you.

the weight of what's gone
jenna lowthert

and before we know it,
*   here we are,*
after so much time has gone by..

wondering how
*   we have survived*
this long without them.

the weight of what's gone
jenna lowthert

i made a wish today.

a wish that you are free
of pain and at peace.

a wish that you would
visit me in my dreams.

a wish that you somehow know
how much I love and miss you.

today, i wished for you.

the weight of what's gone
jenna lowthert

when a person is so important to you,
it is so hard to comprehend the fact that
they are never coming back.

you go to their house and tie up the loose ends.
you struggle to decide what to keep or
what to throw away.

grief is wanting to keep everything that was
ever theirs because sometimes we feel that is
all we have left of them.

but don't forget all of the intangible things
they left behind.

the memories you made together.
the things they have taught you.
the love they left you with.

these things can't be thrown away
because they are forever a part
of your *heart and soul.*

the weight of what's gone
jenna lowthert

when we grieve for a loved one,
we also grieve for ourselves and the
sadness of knowing what we lost.

they're gone, they're not coming back
and *we are left here to miss them.*

the weight of what's gone
jenna lowthert

the empty chair.
the silent room.
all of the words
left unsaid.

grief is the
haunting of
what once was
and what we wish
so badly could
be again.

the weight of what's gone
jenna lowthert

when the seasons change,
i miss you even more
for each thing that changes
is a constant reminder of
time passing by without you here.

the weight of what's gone
jenna lowthert

but maybe
they are
somewhere..

missing us
just as much as
we miss them.

the weight of what's gone
jenna lowthert

"how are you doing?"

    that's a loaded question
    when we are grieving..

where do we even begin?

the weight of what's gone
jenna lowthert

i miss you through the happy times.
i miss you through the sad times.
i miss you on the good days.
i miss you on those hard days, too.

i guess i am just always here..
forever missing you.

the weight of what's gone
jenna lowthert

i never truly understood loss
until i sat next to my mom's
hospital bed and begged
for a miracle *that never came.*

the weight of what's gone
jenna lowthert

when we lose someone
that we love so much,
it changes us in ways
we never could imagine.

it's a crush to our souls.

a reminder that life is
fleeting and fragile,
and that love can be
both beautiful & painful

all at once.

the weight of what's gone
jenna lowthert

we replay our last words
over and over again.

always wishing for just one
more chance to hear their voice
and i don't think that the
longing to speak to them,
just one more time,
ever truly goes away.

the weight of what's gone
jenna lowthert

some losses change
our entire world

forever.

the weight of what's gone
jenna lowthert

i still remember
standing in our old kitchen
thinking to myself that you
would never cook here again.

you would never sit in that spot
on the couch that you always
claimed as yours.

you would never brush your hair
in that bathroom mirror again.

and i would never again hear those
footsteps coming down those stairs
from your bedroom.

i still remember thinking
how unfair it is..

*all the simple things
that you would never
get to do again.*

the weight of what's gone
jenna lowthert

wherever you may be..
a part of me will always
           be there, too.

the weight of what's gone
jenna lowthert

grief is the shadow that follows
you around everywhere you go.

   some days it is barely there.
      some days it is all you can see.

the weight of what's gone
jenna lowthert

when we have
to say goodbye
to someone we love,
we aren't just saying
goodbye to them..

we are saying goodbye
to our future lives that
we *never imagined* them
not being a part of.

the weight of what's gone
jenna lowthert

i will never forget you,
      how could i?

the weight of what's gone
jenna lowthert

you are the beat of my heart.
you are the unseen push in the right direction.
you are the light at the end of every dark day.
it reminds me that you never really left my side.

the weight of what's gone
jenna lowthert

say their name.

shout it from a rooftop.
talk about them. tell their story.
drive with the windows down,
blasting their old favorite songs.
celebrate their life. live yours for them.

never let them be forgotten..
and they will always be remembered.

the weight of what's gone
jenna lowthert

they say that grief is
the price we pay for love..

but what they don't tell you
is that sometimes the cost is so
high that we never truly recover.

the weight of what's gone
jenna lowthert

i always find myself
thinking of the little moments.

the laughter. the love.
when just being together
was enough.

those moments and memories
are all i have left of you..

and that right there is
my saving grace.

the weight of what's gone
jenna lowthert

repeat after me:

this is *my grief journey*
and nobody else's.

i will never allow anyone
to put a timeline on my grief.

i will *never* feel bad for having
a day when i scream and cry
and let it all out.

i will *never* be guilted into
missing my loved one any less
just because so much time
has gone by.

and i will never, ever
stop talking about them
just because people think
that i should be "over it by now"

the weight of what's gone
jenna lowthert

i will always miss you
more than i did yesterday
but never more than
i will tomorrow,
for my life is consumed
by the thought that we
should have had so much
more time together and
i will never go a day
without you on my mind.

the weight of what's gone
jenna lowthert

i still haven't found the exact words
to express just how much i miss you.

it's a heartache that hangs around
and wishing you were here is now
a part of my everyday routine.

the weight of what's gone
jenna lowthert

if you are struggling,
please remember this..

grief is never a sign
of weakness.

grief means we had a
life filled with love.

grief is the way we honor
that love that we still have
in our hearts *for those we lost.*

the weight of what's gone
jenna lowthert

grief and regret
go hand in hand.

all the what ifs.
all the i should haves.

they will drive you mad.

the weight of what's gone
jenna lowthert

i am reminded of you in
the voices of strangers
that sound like you.

in the familiar scent of
the places we used to go.
in the songs that play
at the perfect timing.

you are somehow
everywhere that i am
in the moments when
i need it the most

and i think that in those
moments i am meant to
be reminded of you
because your soul knows
just how much i miss you.

the weight of what's gone
jenna lowthert

honoring you,
even in your absence,
is my way of keeping you alive.

your memory will always live on
in the countless ways you have
touched my heart and soul.

the weight of what's gone
jenna lowthert

heavens gain was
    my hearts biggest loss.

the weight of what's gone
jenna lowthert

you were here one second
*   and then you were gone the next.*

my mind still has a hard time accepting that.

the weight of what's gone
jenna lowthert

how lovely would it be..
to fall asleep and wake up
only to realize that this was

      all just a bad dream.

the weight of what's gone
jenna lowthert

in life and beyond,
*　our bond remains unbreakable.*

the weight of what's gone
jenna lowthert

while the world sleeps,
    my heart weeps

  for you

    and all you
      have missed.

the weight of what's gone
jenna lowthert

losing a parent is not
just a moment of sadness.

it's a lifelong adjustment to
our world as we always knew it

now forever changed.

the weight of what's gone
jenna lowthert

we are so many worlds apart
but your presence still stands
in all the beautiful things
you left behind.

the weight of what's gone
jenna lowthert

and sometimes
the missing them
hurts more than
the saying goodbye.

the weight of what's gone
jenna lowthert

i look to the sky and think of you
and i know that if you can..

you are thinking of me, too.

the weight of what's gone
jenna lowthert

the battle of feeling
like we have to let go
but knowing that we
will forever try to
hold on to it all..

this is grief.

the weight of what's gone
jenna lowthert

*your memory will always
    be the heartbeat of my soul.*

the weight of what's gone
jenna lowthert

grief can be so dark and lonely.

it's a shadow that swallows
every little bit of light.

it leaves you searching for
pieces of yourself that you're
not even sure exist anymore.

it's a heaviness that weighs
you down, making even the
sunniest of days feel so
cloudy and dim..

and it feels like no one can
reach you in that darkness
because *only you know* the
truth depths of what you
have lost.

the weight of what's gone
jenna lowthert

my heart is banking
on the fact that i will
see you again..

    i have to.

the weight of what's gone
jenna lowthert

think of me
but not always with sadness.

think of me and all the moments we shared.
i live in your heart. i will always be there.

smile for me when you see those stars in the sky,
i spend my days watching you from way up high.

think of me in the moments that make your heart soar.
through the joy in your life, remember me more.

dry those tears and clear your view.

look for me in the little things i left behind,
they will always be a part of you.

when you think of me, please don't think of me in sorrow.
i will be with you for all your tomorrows.

for in this life, we are intertwined..

forever through our hearts and minds.

the weight of what's gone
jenna lowthert

not even time can erase
the heartache of what we lost.

the weight of what's gone
jenna lowthert

every sky. every song.

though you have left,
you can't really be gone.

you're in everything..
every word. every sky
every star. every song.

in my heart, your love will reside
a bond like ours, not time, distance,
nor death can divide.

my tears fall like rain
upon the trees,
i look around and
i always find you within me.

the weight of what's gone
jenna lowthert

*i think that when it is
all said and done..*

*after we lay them to rest
and the people start to leave.*

*the flowers start to wilt,
and the sympathy cards stop coming.*

*the check-ins lessen and the world
just keeps on turning..*

*it's like they die all over again
and i think a piece of us dies with them.*

the weight of what's gone
jenna lowthert

on those days when grief
asks too much of you..

it's okay to tell people that
you need time and space.

it's okay to cry your heart
out alone in your room.

it's okay to scream at the top
of your lungs and let it out.

it's okay to do what you need to do
to make it through these days.

the weight of what's gone
jenna lowthert

and i wonder if
it will always feel
as if it were just
yesterday…

*no matter how
many years go by.*

the weight of what's gone
jenna lowthert

though they no longer walk beside you,
let their memory light your way.

let the love they left behind
guide you on your darkest of days.

let their legacy live on through you
and all that you remember them for.

the weight of what's gone
jenna lowtheri

do you ever have one of those moments when you're out shopping, and you catch a quick glimpse of someone who looks like them?

or you hear someone speak and you swear it was their voice that you heard?

then you take a closer look, stare awkwardly for a moment and you realize it's just your mind playing tricks on you..

but for that one split second you felt like they were there with you and in a weird way you want to reach out and hug that person solely based on the fact that they reminded you of them.

the weight of what's gone
jenna lowthert

our hearts shatter from
    the weight that grief puts on it.

we carry a sadness so heavy
    it feels as though it may never lift.

the weight of what's gone
jenna lowthert

grief leaves us with the
constant thought that we
will never see them again
but the hope that, maybe,
one day..

we actually will.

the weight of what's gone
jenna lowthert

maybe all of those stars
    shining up in that sky
are the glowing hearts of those we lost
    shining their light and love on us.

the weight of what's gone
jenna lowthert

the hardest part wasn't just the loss..
it was the learning to live without them
in a place that *doesn't feel like home anymore.*

the weight of what's gone
jenna lowthert

there are moments when i still
reach for the phone to call you..

just to hear your voice.

but i know that if i did,
it wouldn't be you on the other end..

and it hurts all over again.

i hate that you're not here.
i hate that i can't hug you.
i hate that i can't tell you
all about my days.

i always find myself wishing
for one more moment with you.

once more chance to tell you
just how much i love you.

one more laugh at all the things
that only we thought were funny..

and it hurts all over again.

the weight of what's gone
jenna lowthert

how sad it is..

they are here and
then they are gone.

their things left behind.
untouched and unchanged.

their clothes still
hang in their closet.

their toothbrush
still sits unused near
that bathroom sink.

their favorite coffee mug,
still there in that kitchen cabinet.

how sad it is..

these things that were once
a part of their everyday life
are now just reminders of the
person who once used them..

telling a story of who they were,
even after they're gone.

the weight of what's gone
jenna lowthert

i don't think that there
is one single thing
in this entire world
that can prepare us
for having to live
this life without
our parents.

the weight of what's gone
jenna lowthert

grief is like a mountain, so high and steep.
an endless path that never fails to make us weep.

it's shadow towers in the dark night..
such a heavy burden, with its never-ending height.

each step we take, a painful climb..
through all the love left in the stones of time.

we stumble on our rocks of sorrow,
always wondering how we will make it
through tomorrow?

the top seems so very far away yet we still find
the strength to climb the uneven terrain.

grief is like a mountain. it's a test of our will.
this journey can be both relentless and still.

but in the sadness and heartache we feel on our climb..

we find the resilience of our hearts and our minds.

the weight of what's gone
jenna lowthert

when we lose a parent,
we don't just lose a loved one.

we lose all we have ever known.

the ones who raised us to
be who we are today.

a vital piece of our world goes
missing and we ache for it back.

and no matter how old we are,
we still feel so lost without them..

we still need them.

but through their loss, the strength
we show on our grief journey is
the reminder of the influence that
they continue to have on our lives..

and always will.

the weight of what's gone
jenna lowthert

*i wish i had wings so
i could fly up to heaven
to tell you how much
i have missed you.*

the weight of what's gone
jenna lowthert

death can't be final..

because a bond like ours
can never be broken.

i must believe that
i will see you again..

someday.
someway.
somehow.

the weight of what's gone
jenna lowthert

the clock ticks.
the time moves on.
but for some of us
it stands still..

we get stuck in the
moment when we last
saw their face..

and i think a part of us
wants to stay in that moment,
because as sad as it was..

at least we were still with them.

the weight of what's gone
jenna lowthert

she wasn't just my mother.
she was so much more than that.

she was the true embodiment of love.

she was the best friend who stood
by my side no matter what.

she's the one who loved me
without condition and i wouldn't
be half the person i am today
if it weren't for her and
all she has shown me.

the weight of what's gone
jenna lowthert

i reach for the phone to call,
like i always used to do.

for one single split second,
i forgot that you wouldn't
be on the other end.

then i remember..
and the silence
is louder than
any sound that
i've ever heard.

the weight of what's gone
jenna lowtheri

to my grieving daughter,

i hope the days you have spent without me have
not been filled with so much heartache and sadness.
i hope they have been filled with all the love, strength,
and happiness you deserve. though i am no longer with
you on earth, please know that i am always watching
over you, i have not missed a beat. this life is filled with
ups and downs and i know you've struggled with my
passing but i hope you continue to live your life in the
fullest way possible. life is a gift and i want you to
always remember to make the most of it. love life, go see
the world, always be kind to others and never give up on
those dreams of yours. when you are sad, please
remember that you always carry a piece of me with you.
we are forever connected, no matter the distance.

you have my heart; you are my heart.

when you feel lost or lonely, please think of me with joy
rather than sadness, and when you are missing me,
please think of all the happy times, the laughter, and the
love that we shared. i know i can't be by your side to tell
you that it will all be okay, but you must know, my
daughter, that my love for you never went away. never
forget that i live in your heart and one day, when the
time is right, i will see you again and hug you so tight.

with all my love from heaven,

mom

the weight of what's gone
jenna lowthert

the second you died,
i knew that i would
miss you for the rest of my life.

the weight of what's gone
jenna lowthert

you were the best of the best.
you were the heart of our family.
you were the rock that we stood on.
you were the glue that held it all together.

and nothing has been the same
without you.

the weight of what's gone
jenna lowthert

when you lose a parent,
you lose the person who knew you
before you even knew yourself.

a piece of your past goes with them..

and a piece of your future, too.

the weight of what's gone
jenna lowthert

i hope you are
    watching me
from above
and so proud of
    the person
i've become.

the weight of what's gone
jenna lowthert

we are stuck somewhere
    in the middle of what was
          and *what remains.*

the weight of what's gone
jenna lowthert

i still remember walking down
that sad, dark hallway of the hospital
feeling as if i was leaving you behind
and when I reached those doors,
i stepped outside, and in that moment
i knew that my life *would never
be the same again..*

and even after all these years, i still hope
*you knew that I never wanted to leave
your side.*

the weight of what's gone
jenna lowthert

i hate the month of may
and that feeling that i get
when spring approaches.

the flowers start to bloom.
the sun starts to stay.

and while the world
around me sings..

i still mourn the loss
that may brought to me.

the weight of what's gone
jenna lowthert

it's so hard to say goodbye
        to the life we lived
                before they died.

the weight of what's gone
jenna lowthert

but what if i did get one
more moment with you?

would it be enough or
would i always wish
for just one more?

the weight of what's gone
jenna lowthert

the loss of someone we love
is a story we carry with us
for the rest of our lives.

it becomes a part of who we are
and it shapes the way we navigate
this world without them.

the weight of what's gone
jenna lowthert

the stars remind me of you.
so bright, so beautiful.

yet so far away.

the weight of what's gone
jenna lowthert

they live on through us.
through the things that we do.
through the stories that we tell.
through the love we still hold for them.

they are forever a part of us
and we are forever a part of them.

the weight of what's gone
jenna lowthert

i hope that wherever you are,
there is no pain or sadness.

i hope that you are happy and free.

i hope that you somehow know how
loved you still are and *always will be.*

the weight of what's gone
jenna lowthert

from your dad in heaven

to my daughter,

my wish for you is that you are embraced in all the light and love that this world has to offer. although you can no longer see me, i want you to know that i am still very much a part of your life, forever watching you from the sky. please remember that i have loved every precious moment that i had with you, my sweet daughter. i am so lucky to be your dad. i am your guardian angel now, always protecting you just as i did on earth. when you find yourself missing me, i hope you look to your heart because that is where you will find me. i have left all the best pieces of me with you and i know you will use them to look ahead to the brighter days. never forget that you are strong enough to make it through any storm that comes your way. i am with you through every struggle, every sorrow and every happy moment. take some time to stop and look around at all the beauty that still remains. never stop dreaming and always share your love with the world, just as you shared it with me.

you will always be my little girl,

dad

the weight of what's gone
jenna lowthert

i miss you..

very, very,
very, very,
very, very,
very, very,
very, very,
very, very,
very, very,
very, very,
very, very,
very much.

the weight of what's gone
jenna lowthert

you don't fully
understand grief
until you lose
someone you
love deeply..

even then,

there are still so
   many questions.

the weight of what's gone
jenna lowthert

to all of those who
so desperately fought
the hardest fight to save
your loved one's life.

to have to helplessly
watch them slip away.

to be told that there is
nothing more that
can be done.

to have to make decisions
that no person should ever
have to make and to have
sleepless nights thinking
about it all…

i see you. i understand you.

i am you.

the weight of what's gone
jenna lowthert

time slips through our fingers,
leaving us with the ache of wondering
what we should have done with every second,
if we had only known, that in that moment

those were our last seconds.

the weight of what's gone
jenna lowthert

i can't see you..
    but i can still love you.

the weight of what's gone
jenna lowthert

on our darkest days of grief
we find ourselves facing a
void that can never be filled.

do we even want it to be?

that void in your heart is reserved
for the one that you lost and that's okay.

it is the only space where they can forever stay.

the weight of what's gone
jenna lowthert

i don't have all the answers
and i can't tell you why they
were taken from you.

i can't fix your broken heart and
i can't make your sadness disappear.

i can't promise you that tomorrow
will be better and i won't lie to you
and tell you that grief goes away.

but what i will tell you is that you is that
you are here. you are alive. you can make
sure that they are never forgotten.

make that your mission. make them proud.
honor the life that they loved to live.

live your life for the ones you love
who no longer can.

the weight of what's gone
jenna lowthert

in the moment when
someone we love dies...

time stands still for us.

the clock stops ticking.

but the rest of the world
just keeps on going.

would it be easier if
the entire universe
could just pause for
a moment and
mourn beside us?

the weight of what's gone
jenna lowthert

when you miss me, close your eyes..
feel the warmth of that beautiful sunrise.
i am the light that shines upon your face,
forever holding you in an unseen embrace.

when you miss me, listen for that breeze..
hear my laughter in the falling leaves.

i am in every single song that plays,
listen to them to get through your days.

when you miss me, look up to that night sky.
i am the star that's shining from way up high.

i am in your heart, where i have always been..
forever a part of you, always deep within.

when you miss me, please know that i am near,
i am in every smile and i am in every tear.

i will be with you in every way and my love
still surrounds you through all of your days.

the weight of what's gone
jenna lowthert

and then there are the people
who stick by your side through
all the heartache of grief..

the ones who know your heart.

they don't try to fix your pain,
they don't try to come up with
the perfect words to say..

they are just there, *beside you.*

they show up and sit with you in silence.

proof that even through death,
love is still very much alive all around you.

they remind you that you don't have
to carry this heaviness alone.

these are the people you will never forget.

the weight of what's gone
jenna lowthert

we have so much left to say to them,
even when we think we said it all.

we are left here with a
heart full of *unspoken words.*

the weight of what's gone
jenna lowthert

we may be weathered..
but we are *not broken.*

the weight of what's gone
jenna lowthert

they say that grief is
the price we pay for love
and i think i would pay it
a thousand times over
if it meant that i could
hug you one more time

the weight of what's gone
jenna lowthert

i miss you in the quiet moments
i miss you in the loud ones, too..

and every moment in between.

the weight of what's gone
jenna lowthert

i find you
in the ocean waves
crashing on the sand.
in every beautiful sunset
that never fails to meet land.
i find you in the autumn leaves
falling to the ground,
in every bird that stops by,
but never makes a sound.
i find you on those back roads
that we used to love to drive.
i find you when the snowflakes
fall from that cold winter sky.
i find you in the springtime,
when the flowers start to bloom.
i find you in my heart, where for you,
i will always hold room.

i find you in every day
and in every beautiful place.

i find you in every song,
every season, every sky
and in every space.

wherever my eyes wander,
i am forever finding you,
in all the little things that
you used to love to do.

the weight of what's gone
jenna lowthert

losing someone you love
   is like watching the sunset
      and knowing that it will never
         rise in the same way again.

the weight of what's gone
jenna lowthert

*the depth of our grief
 measures the magnitude
    of our love.*

the weight of what's gone
jenna lowthert

grief is so sneaky.

one minute you're fine,
the next minute you're in
the aisle of a grocery store
crying because you saw
a snack they used to love.

the weight of what's gone
jenna lowthert

from the second you
took your last breath,
i knew that i would
miss you forever.

your loss has left a
tremendous void that
nothing could *ever* fill.

the weight of what's gone
jenna lowthert

all of the things we
will never get to do..

that is what breaks
my heart in two.

the weight of what's gone
jenna lowthert

grief is not just a passing emotion.

it is a permanent scar on our hearts.

*it's the constant reminder of what we lost
but it's also a tribute to the love that lives
on despite of how deep that pain goes.*

the weight of what's gone
jenna lowthert

they say that "time heals all wounds"
but i have never believed that to be true.

time forces us to live in our "new normal"
where we are expected to heal quickly.

times means nothing when the ones
we love are no longer here with us..

missing them is a forever kind of thing.

the weight of what's gone
jenna lowthert

*and i can't help but wonder
what life would be like if you
were still here.*

the weight of what's gone
jenna lowthert

you are gone
but your love
is still felt
in every crack
of my bruised
and broken heart.

the weight of what's gone
jenna lowthert

one thing that
i miss the most
is being able
to call you
just to chat.

the weight of what's gone
jenna lowthert

you never really realize how
much you can miss someone..

until you miss them.

the weight of what's gone
jenna lowthert

just in case nobody told you..

you are stronger than you think you are.
your heart is more resilient than you know.
you are doing the best you can..

& that is okay.

the weight of what's gone
jenna lowthert

we dwell so much on
the fact that they died
that we sometimes must
force ourselves not to
forget that they lived,

for their life gave us such
beautiful, unforgettable
moments and memories.

the weight of what's gone
jenna lowthert

if you're going to tell me that
everything happens for a reason..

i hope you are able to tell me
what that reason was.

the weight of what's gone
jenna lowthert

i'm still here,
even if you cannot see me.

i send you little signs—
look around, *they're everywhere.*

that song that always randomly
plays when you're feeling sad.

that cardinal in your yard that
always seems to come back.

that dream that felt
too real to ignore.

pay attention..

that's me,
reminding you,
that i am closer
than you think.

the weight of what's gone
jenna lowthert

through grief we learn
that time, *unfortunately,*
waits for no one.

the weight of what's gone
jenna lowthert

grief is such a thief.

the weight of what's gone
jenna lowthert

when my grandmother,
who i had such a close bond with,
was towards the end of her life..
a friend of hers asked for an update.

i told him that she is just *so tired.*

not tired in a sleepy way, but tired of
the fight she had to put up to stay alive..

he replied with

"i don't think any of us
can comprehend being tired,
in this context, until perhaps
one day we are faced
with it ourselves."

*..and that will stick with me
for the rest of my life.*

the weight of what's gone
jenna lowthert

the time just
keeps flying by..

like it's trying
to outrun the
heartache of
missing you.

the weight of what's gone
jenna lowthert

after my mom died, i remember thinking
often about how we could ever leave this house.
how could we possibly bag up her things,
get rid of them, and just leave that house behind?

is a house really a home when your loved one is gone?

no…it's not.

a house, in fact, is just a house.

just because that house is the only place i've ever
known her, doesn't change the fact that she's gone.
leaving there didn't make me love or miss her any less.

as much as i would love to hold onto every single
thing forever, i know that i can't..

and what i've come to realize is that just because we
move forward with our lives, does not mean that we
forget them.

and as hard as it was for me to leave that house,
the only place that i have ever called home..

i now know that a house is just a house.

it's the people that make it a home.

the weight of what's gone
jenna lowthert

close your eyes for a minute..

imagine it's a warm summer day.

your loved ones who have passed on
are still alive and healthy.

your entire family is together,
laughing and living..

just like you used to do.

in that minute.. life is so good.

the weight of what's gone
jenna lowthert

grief teaches us
that healing has
nothing to do with
erasing the pain.

it's about finding
ways to live with it,
ways to carry it even
when our hearts are
hurting.

*it's about finding new
ways to live in honor
of the ones we lost.*

the weight of what's gone
jenna lowthert

sometimes we have
these moments in life
that no matter how long ago,
we remember so vividly..
as if it just happened.

maybe this is our minds
way of taking a picture.

maybe these moments aren't
meant to be forgotten, no matter
how hard they are to remember.

the weight of what's gone
jenna lowthert

losing you was like
walking in a world
that has lost every
bit of its color.

the weight of what's gone
jenna lowthert

yes, life goes on.
but it's a *different* one now.

the weight of what's gone
jenna lowthert

the world still turns.
the sun still shines.
but it is never quite as
warm as it once was.

the weight of what's gone
jenna lowthert

we never stop wanting
to make them proud…

    even when they are no
    longer here anymore.

the weight of what's gone
jenna lowthert

i didn't lose you all at once.

as time moves on,
i realize that i lose you
piece by piece.

day by day.

year by year.

all the countless moments
when i find myself forgetting
the way your voice sounded,
the way you said my name,
or the way it felt to be near you..

it's the longest and the hardest goodbye.

the weight of what's gone
jenna lowthert

i carry this
homesickness
deep within
my heart.

wherever i may go,
nothing *will ever*
feel like home
without you.

the weight of what's gone
jenna lowthert

no matter how
much time passes,
no matter how much
i age and become older.

a part of me will
always be that girl
reaching out for
my mother that
*i will never stop
needing.*

the weight of what's gone
jenna lowthert

you're gone, but i still have
so much left to say to you.

you're gone, but there are so
many things we still had to do.

you're gone, but this life just
isn't the same without you..

you're gone, but the only person
who could make me feel better..

is you.

the weight of what's gone
jenna lowthert

the leaves start to fall,
there is a chill in the air.

i feel the weight of missing you,
even more than i usually do.

because as these seasons change..

it reminds me that some things
are gone forever

no matter how many times
this world renews itself.

the weight of what's gone
jenna lowthert

life moves forward,
but part of me is still
holding on to you.

your absence is heavy,
but so is the love you
left behind..

and that's what keeps me going.

the weight of what's gone
jenna lowthert

i think of all
that has changed..

*so much of it
has changed.*

but so much has
remained the same..

like how the sun
never fails to set.

like how the flowers
never fail to bloom.

like how the sky can
still look so pretty,

*even when our
hearts are so sad.*

the weight of what's gone
jenna lowthert

one day they're here,
laughing and living.

and then in an instant
they are gone.

just like that.

it has always shocked me..
how quickly *someone can
become a memory.*

the weight of what's gone
jenna lowthert

some days are still so sad.
some days i feel at peace.

but one thing always remains..

i miss you fiercely and i always will.

the weight of what's gone
jenna lowthert

i hope you know
that you are *never* alone.

i hope you know that there
are so many others who have
walked this path before you..

ones who understand your pain.

ones who understand that there is
an ache that never seems to go away.

ones who truly understand
the weight of what is gone.

i hope you find peace.

i hope you let their memory
become the source of your strength,
the bittersweet reminder that although
they no longer walk this earth..

they will forever be a part of you
and you will forever be a part of them.

the weight of what's gone
jenna lowthert

the weight of what's gone
jenna lowthert

IF YOU'RE LOST, COME FOLLOW ME

FACEBOOK	INSTAGRAM

TIKTOK	WEBSITE

the weight of what's gone
jenna lowthert

MY OTHER BOOKS

LIFE GOES ON..?

LIFE STILL GOES ON..
THE BLOGBOOK OF A
MOTHERLESS DAUGHTER

the weight of what's gone
jenna lowthert

the weight of what's gone
jenna lowthert

in memory of my mom, gina.

10/30/1964 – 05/27/2013

the weight of what's gone
jenna lowthert

the weight of what's gone
jenna lowthert

THE WEIGHT
OF WHAT'S GONE

www.daughterofanangel.com

-

Copyright © 2024 Jenna Lowthert

All rights reserved.

No part of this publication may be reproduced, stored or transmitted in any form or by any means, electronic, mechanical, photocopying, recording, scanning, or otherwise without written permission from the publisher. It is illegal to copy this book, post it to a website, or distribute it by any other means without permission.

Jenna Lowthert asserts the moral right to be identified as the sole author of this work.

-

ISBN: 9798338660270

Printed in Great Britain
by Amazon